The Beauty V

C000128174

THE BEAUTY WITHIN SHADOW

Henry Normal

Flapjack Press
www.flapjackpress.co.uk

Exploring the synergy between performance and the page

Published in 2020 by Flapjack Press
Salford, Gtr Manchester
⊕ flapjackpress.co.uk
f Flapjack Press   🐦 FlapjackPress

ISBN 978-1-9161479-0-4

Cover art by Johnny Carroll-Pell
f Art By Johnny   © johnnycarrollpell
Photographs courtesy of the author

Printed by Imprint Digital
Upton Pyne, Exeter, Devon
⊕ digital.imprint.co.uk

City of Literature

*I'd like to dedicate this book to
my two younger sisters, Valerie and Angela.
Both are glorious forces of nature.*

I would like to thank Linda Hallam, Theresa Sowerby, Paul Neads, Penny Shepherd and my wife Angela Pell for their help in bringing this collection together.

Contents

Official introduction

Please welcome tonight's poet...

The 2019 winner of the coveted Ted Hughes Award
isn't him

The winner of this year's National Poetry Competition
is somebody completely different

Tonight's poet is not the winner of any award named after any
dead poet nor any award sponsored by a coffee chain nor given
by some people in a small Welsh town

In 2017 he didn't win some obscure prize you've never heard of
awarded by some appointed (or self-appointed) judges you've
never heard of

He has not been awarded honours of any description
by a monarch of any description

and has not been authorised to put three letters after his name
for basically doing the job he's paid to do

In 2019 he wasn't named 'Professor of Poetry'
at a prestigious university
2020 same
2021 don't hold your breath

To be honest I don't know why he bothered turning up
Ladies and gentlemen with sincere apologies
Henry Normal (CSE French Grade 3)

The Beauty Within Shadow

The beauty within shadow

There is often light
in the darkness
once your eyes adjust

and when your sight fails
it is said other senses
heighten

even with your lids tight
the mind can shine
like the midday sun

and in the blackest
void who knows
what awaits

maybe another sense rises
to help us become
light ourselves

or returns us to a time
when all was in balance
awaiting ignition

Visually inviting but thermally challenging

Even the word exhilaration
can't capture the joy of the vast ocean
with its overspill gurgling between our toes

Here shale is mined by waves
avalanches replace dynamite
clouds become wisps from God's beard

Nothing but new lands lie out there
beyond the horizon
and the horizon beyond

Whilst all around is movement
we choose to be still

though tied to Earth
we spiral together

accelerating
with the expansion

giddy

A mid-October depression

Rain strums on my window

Outside the dahlias
are under attack

There is nothing I can do
to prevent this

Stems arc
with the bluster

Leaves shiver
parry and deflect

The wind punishes all life
that dares raise itself above ground

Colours in the midst of battle
petals of subdued pink refuse to fall

Under cloud cover
there is still light to be had

Buds yet emerging

The morning after the storm

Over-watered plant pots squat
        surface tension bulging
                at the brim

I lift my bench upright
and place the bird feeder
back on its hook

The sundial casts a solid line
marking
the approach of noon

I am overdressed
in this winter sweater
sweating

The sun
is an open fire
fully drawn

Whatever cloud there is
is wrung dry
and presents no shade

Seaweed and pebbles
carpet the coastal path
Chalk cliffs are scoured clean

Too many people
are out walking too many dogs
for Johnny's liking

White triangles
on fluid blue
catch the leftover breeze

Sleep has seen off rainbows
though each puddle
now shines as liquid gold

In search of the perfect feminine

My wife said
nothing rhymes with orange
but before despair could befall her
I corrected Angela
or Ange
as I call her

The Wasteland 2: *The Sequel – This Time it's Personal*

By the old sewage pipe
we'd hide in tall grasses
and learn what came out
of other folks' asses
and this we'd prefer
to sitting in classes

It is surprising that tiles remain on roofs

Swimming in a sombrero
amid the Christmas rain

a mum with her son
undress for the weather

Swifts accelerate
through rising steam

past lemon trees that border
the far corner of the pool

Palm trees wiggle thin fingers
as their trunks sway in slo-mo

Beyond the olive trees
pearl and silver paint every corner

Against aquamarine tiles
a pink bathing costume itself

would usually be enough
to draw your eye

Free verse at discount prices

"There's no money in poetry, but then there's no poetry in money either"
– Robert Graves

There's no big bucks in poetry books
No budgetary boom with a slim volume

The general rule is –
no spondoolies

No career's crueller
for lack of moolah

The weight of wampum will underwhelm
Royalties appear only in the quantum realm

The financial projection for a new collection
will hardly evoke an instant erection

Fat cats and poesy
don't sit that cosy

The gist of it –
you make jack shit

You'll e'er be near John Clare
far from Lord Byron or a billionaire

Yes to tender words – but no legal tender
It's less Johnny Cash more Stephen Spender

To expect literary lolly is fruitless folly
even with off rhymes, you're off your trolley

Folding green and photos of the queen
in wordsmiths' wallets such wads are seldom seen

It's not the racket to pocket a packet
or put a pretty penny in your poet's purse
Being a bard – banking is hard
There's no blank cheque for blank verse

no bread and jam in an epigram
no chunk of change in a clerihew
a magnum opus is monetarily hopeless
revenue due for new haiku barely a bob or two

You'll not get rich quick with a limerick
not pack a bundle off the back of a rondel
not cement a cent coining a lament
To earn a load from an ode is seldom à la mode

Lidl won't take an idyll
to a tanka – they'll say 'no thankya'
A traditional ballad is also invalid

A rondeau will raise no dough
An epic or lyric – zip zilch zero

However clever your elegy
it'll never a big seller be
you'll ever be the feller with 50p

Each villanelle's a bagatelle
Hell, they just don't sell that well

Savings from a sonnet?
Don't bank on it

Ain't no gold in them thar hills
apart from golden daffodils

Uttering metaphor
is better for
putting the fun into insufficient funds

the wherewithal
to make a withdrawal
is more often moribund

The lure of loads of lucre
you may as well bazooka

Not wishing to come on tactless
poets pursuing profit should pack it in
you'll make sod all contactless
and even less chip and pin

No matter how moving or funny
you'll forever
be financially unsound

Your name'll never
be synonymous with money
unless you're Ezra Pound

The locking knee joint

This simple ball and socket
and the ability to lock it

led, it is said, to becoming a biped
and fed brain-size within the head

This enhanced hinge
upon upright stance did not impinge

It's the linchpin
of the hominin

A unique joint
that would not disappoint

these evolutionary Johnny-come-latelies
between the Tigres and the Euphrates

The sea has shrunk

Pockmarked boulders
harbour rock pools early evening

Sloped sand carries stretch marks
mirrored by clouds scraped south

A fat man in his wetsuit
walks those extra yards

A fisherman on his iPhone
casts his line further

Spindly trees cling to a cliff edge
Signs warn of instability

Seen only in effect
the moon is both light and heavy

Purple seaweed at Porto Moss

Fresh Orange
never even touches
the sides of the straw

as Johnny draws the last drops
sounding like
a cappuccino machine

On the next table
German humanists
enjoy Christmas chips

Outside the sea
keeps doing the business
as does the staff inside

Gulls hover
high above
like speech marks

The sun
is an egg yolk
poaching

Angela's hair
flies sideways
lassoing the clouds

Mussel shells
dot the sand
like full stops

That's got to be some good coffee

My rented Kia plays a little tune
whenever I start or stop the engine

It pips if I cross a white line
and seems desperate for attention

I pull into a space at the supermarket
where even in winter there are witnesses

Near the automatic glass doors
next to two rows of chained trolleys

half a dozen small tables with chairs
sit on tarmac facing the car park

We are two hundred yards
from an uninterrupted view of the ocean

but here under a giant sun screen that casts no shadow
women in sunglasses sip espresso

Shoppers trigger the constant opening and closing
of tall sliding panes (though not as quietly as you'd want)

Unhooking their tinny noisemaker
each passing customer twangs with purpose into the aisles

then exiting with a duller tone
loads their boot with a thud

and discards the wire and castors
as they fart off home

On one of the aluminium tables an old man
with a Van Dyke moustache and beard set

relaxes alone smartly casual
in co-ordinated beige and chalk

smoking an unfiltered cigarette
and blowing grey smoke

shorts or long trousers
a marginal decision today

One old woman wears dark glasses
on top of her white hair

whilst she picks at posh pastry
with a plastic fork

Another pensioner checks her dog is comfy
on its blanket in the back of her estate

A large refrigerated truck throbs
as it manoeuvres to the trade entrance

blocking the less than panoramic view
of the café clientele's own cars

It coughs black clouds
as it dwarfs its surroundings

A huge photo of a chef in his hat
adorns the side of the truck

his hand gesture says 'OK'

Taking the sea air

A mother and daughter
under bubble wrap clouds

arm in arm find equilibrium
not a prescription in sight

From this angle they're only as tall
as a couple of waves

Oxygen surrounds them
inside and out

with close examination of the sand
you can see shadows within footprints

like the indentations where tablets
are removed from a blister

the reflection of a walking stick
appears at a strangely jaunty angle

The sky is Man City at the horizon
Chelsea close to

The sun is filtered
as is recollection

Man
made
strata

mainly flat
by selection

the smallest
towards the top

these stacked stones
seem to defy Newton

but in truth gravity
and friction cement
their position resisting
the testing wind

this material is
pre-laid
pre-lifted
pre-eroded
pre-fallen

limestone rounded
by tide and abrasion
cream or ivory
with hints of slate or rose and
rough broken edges that appear lighter

the shadow of each stack presents as solid
further warped by the undulation of the sand
it contorts into some strange malformed figure
almost human or human kind
growing taller as the sun moves west

Pineapple – perfic on a cocktail stick

Fresh, ring or chunk
never debunk

This tropical delicacy
once incited jealousy

and adorned the plate
of Catherine the Great

A fruit with which to be reckoned
thought Charles II

Brought to Europe by Columbus
at court it caused quite some fuss

The 4th Earl of Dunmore
built a temple in its honour

Sir Christopher Wren
put one of them

on St Paul's south tower
such was the pineapple's power

Its allure still lingers
as a sign for swingers

Upside down in your trolley
says you're up for a jolly

put one at your door
no need to say more

Ironically it's used to tenderise meat
and make seminal fluid sweet

Ananas comosus
from all the best grocers

A fruit of repute
without dispute

The perfect sight
with Angel Delight

and a polite invite
for an interesting night

Life as she is to visit

Tall trees try to pollinate the pool
aided and abetted by the breeze

Small specks too tiny for the net
form a film on the surface

Only the waterfall's edge
can provide a filter

Given the huge number of seeds
the small area of water

the distance from the woods
and the unpredictability of weather

I wonder about
the surrounding wasteland

how with season after season
it's not already covered with conifers

It seems nature is
playing the percentages

Does a baby in the womb dream of I?

I suspect my Dad was lonely
most of his life

I did little to help

I tell myself perfection is singular
imperfection more creative

I strive to be imperfect
in my own unique way

I cling to these lines like a raft
though none will matter in time

I know no-one wants to hear such talk
for fear of the undertow

I believe the only real conversation we have
is with ourselves

I carry this distance
like a silence

I pray for a common-or-garden miracle
like I'm domesticating God

I am still a child running through fountains

Plane language

At the airport Johnny
wears a green lanyard
with bright yellow sunflowers

for people
whose special needs
are not immediately obvious

Six foot three with bright red ear defenders
and chewing a toy nutcracker
you might think his condition was fairly obvious

He follows his grandma
through 'Wheelchair Assisted Boarding'
Her needs are easily assessed

At the baggage check
we put our hand luggage into the plastic tray
ear defenders, lanyard and walking stick in another

The passport officer
assesses if we constitute
a terrorist threat

A grandma recovering from heart attack and stroke
A partially deaf granddad on Statins
A 'mildly severe' autistic 21year old

A mother so tired her heart is erratic
and a lightweight poet with pretensions
After due consideration he lets us through

Those who have paid for priority boarding
attempt to assert
their natural air of entitlement

Standing as close to the barriers as possible
their boarding passes on iPhones they remind me
cocky is never a good look

Fingers crossed
there are no babies on the seats in front
behind or to the side of us

Angela's prepared Johnny's usual snacks
bacon, jam sandwich, apple and crisps
all part of the routine coping strategy

Thank goodness we're not on the seats
next to the emergency door
or we'd be made to move

The announcer asks if we can refrain
from eating nuts or nut-based foods
as someone on board has a nut allergy

If they'd had a bacon allergy
they'd be in trouble
There's no stopping Johnny eating that

I wonder
if the person concerned has a lanyard
and what pictures are on it

**Treatise on the social discourse concerning
council housing in the 1960s and '70s
addressed to the child of a private property owner**

As a kid what I remember most
is I had a place to call home

A bloke from the council painted our door
and you had to paint your own

The attraction of proximity

Lying low on my
sun lounger I almost hug
the ground – perspective

like a racing car
making the experience
more immediate

The westernmost branches of the cherry blossom are becoming bare

I click my pen
like the ticking of a time piece

A framed photo sits
on the window ledge

a young soul
long departed

her hand to her cheek
her wristwatch in evidence

The clock-face is angled
It's not possible to see how late it is

I don't know this woman
only her descendants

her DNA merged with mine
as part of my son

His photo sits alongside
as we share these seconds

On the outside of the pane
the rain slows

The pause between drips
becomes longer

Elpis within the jar

My car throbs
like an old tractor
or a faulty spin dryer

Three-point turns
inscribe the snow
as Spirograph

Rain
dilutes winter
into a flavourless Slushy

One of these poems will be my last
although of no more significance
than any other

Somewhere along the way
someone seems to have
lost something

My wife hates these lines
and tells me darkness
is upsetting in those you love

The sun and the clouds
conspire
to cast shapes on the sea

One of these breaths will be my last
although of no more significance
than any other

If I stand back
from my screen
I fear the next line

A skin tent held by brittle bones
I long to find a new truth
that I can tell myself

I cling to the thought
that Elpis within the jar
is still Elpis

One part of me is slimming (with a northern accent)

My brain is not getting fatter
I'm losing white and grey matter
especially the latter
containing essential 'datter'

Yet slimming is meant to flatter
so goes the patter
a myth I easily shatter
as memories scatter

I'm mad as a hatter
putting my faith in 'watter'
and an oily fish platter
and a purple sweet 'po-tatter'

When you're not even the best at coming last

Love your inner loser
be a winner refuser
a short-comings chooser
not an imperfection excuser

Say no to ego playing the victim
contradict him, be strict, evict him
This is only how you've picked
to depict him

Don't veil your pale allure
nail your failure for sure
pray it prevails ever more
never procure some fairy tale cure

All also-rans lord your lacking
sack attacking achievement-slacking
make mistakes with no back tracking
guilt and regret can both get packing

Never retreat from being beat
never bleat about the balance sheet
each setback you meet is sweet
without defeat life's incomplete

Celebrate this lack of success
Mess in Progress – no stress
To being human let's confess
am I a fuck up? – Hell yes

With Michael Mitchell in mid-July

We are bathed in sunshine
surrounded by picnickers
using the trees as marquees

The church is at our back
the cemetery gates open
Dogs yelp for attention

Summer dresses
and collapsible chairs
find some use at last

Cigarettes
and vapes
are kept to the outskirts

A middle-aged man
wears his cap back to front
and holds a skateboard

His wife has dyed blue and green hair
Older men wear pastel shirts
not a collar in sight

Occasional clouds hurry to reach Seaford
Their shadows skim the warm grass
up into the fields and over the oaks

A line of boulders prevents access to cars
though could be mistaken
for having other significance

Michael would be 82 if he was still alive
What would he make of it all I wonder
He died a year younger than I am now

A weather vane on the spire
points in the opposite direction
to the prevailing wind

Haiku 575

There's more to haiku
than counting syllables but
not so with this one

Clumsy verse

Metre and rhyme
are fine
for comic time-
ing

but if serious stuff etc
is your raison d'être
free verse is better-
er

There was a young man from Nantucket

There was a young man from Nantucket
who loved blank verse

A happy accident

Retracing our steps
past the covered boats

along the beach east
to where the heron still rests

our son's tracks are easy to spot
heavy on the toes

Yours are smaller
and spread more evenly

The tread of my Doc Martens
looks at odds

like an astronaut
on the lunar surface

I pick up two pairs of sandals
from the flat rock

and head back
this time alone

The sun ready to dip
The sea changing colour

Salema in the distance
bathed in a Christmas light

like Bethlehem-on-Sea

Poem for those who inadvertently forgot to buy a book during the interval

I blame myself
I'm not sure I mentioned I had books for sale

enough

No – it's a simple fact
the quality of the poetry in the first half obviously failed
to entice a purchase

This is awkward

Perhaps it's best if I don't draw attention to the matter

I realise of course
it's not necessarily an insult
as such

no more than say the lack of a compliment

Perhaps some people
are waiting for the end of the show proper
weighing up their options
as to which book or books
would suit them best

No, this is awkward

It's not as though I need the money
which probably makes it more awkward

The thought that people could sit there
and watch me read my poetry

laugh with me
maybe fight back the odd tear
but not be moved to want to own a memento
a remembrance
for a mere £10.00
is too hard to bear

Maybe these people have bought
all my books already

But they couldn't have bought my new collection
it's only just been released

Maybe they've pre-ordered it on the internet
that's 'how big a fan they are'

and they'd have brought it here tonight
for me to sign
but they're too awestruck

Probably not

I should just carry on with the second half
as though nothing has happened

the last thing I want is
awkwardness

It's not personal
it's purely business
or lack of business in this case

I'll simply entertain these ingrates
like in the first half
but with even more quality
especially of the 'book-purchase-enticing' kind

I know it's vanity
pure vanity
on their part

but I refuse to lower myself
They're just needy
There I've said it
it's quite unattractive

What I'll do is
I'll express myself honestly
through my art
but secretly I'll pity them
for their poverty
either spiritual or financial

Wait a minute
maybe these people are destitute
and could only scrimp and save
and scrape together enough money for tonight's ticket
going without food
or chancing eviction by using their rent money
desperate
in the hope of instilling some much needed
top quality poetry
into their pitiful lives

Maybe they'd have definitely bought a book
but they've taken out a short-term high interest loan
to buy their ticket for tonight
which they've no way of repaying
and are destined to have their furniture repossessed
or their legs broken

Oh I do hope so

The less said the better

To those reading these poems after my death

Don't be put off
by my demise

At the point
of writing these poems
I was
of course
very much alive

These are not
the words of a dead man
talking to other dead men

but the perceptions
of a living mind
concerned with pain
and love and all things
vital and immediate

This poetry is perhaps
the best of
what was once me

It's only
I've since retired
from writing

at least
for now

Sonnet zero

with thanks to Elizabeth Barrett Browning

How do I love thee? let me count the ways –
none, nil, nana, on no account, noways

not a touch, a tad, a trace
not a dab, a dram, a dash
I hate your stupid lying face
it's a face I'd like to smash

nothing doing, not a smidgen
hating you's my new religion

not a spot, a speck, a shred
I'd laugh a lot if you were dead

no small change, no small beer
you need no ready reckoner here

A whole lot of not a jot
is the love for you I've got
to hit the spot I hope you rot

not a bean
not in the least
less than the number
of the beast

no need for calculators
no need to draw a graph
no need to catch you later
you can do the math

not a crumb – the total sum
not a soupçon – it's all gone

work this out in calculus
there's one me and none of us

it all adds up to less than nought
value of the negative sort

zero's not quite the right vicinity
my love for you is minus infinity

To join with gold (kintsugi)

Broken many times
We've been put back together
now better than new

Joins tell the story
of how we learn to become
mag nif i cen t

Persian flaw

I love the idea
of deliberately making
something imperfect

Invocation of the nine daughters of Zeus and Mnemosyne

The number and the names of the Muses
may be unknown to you

but you build a shrine to them
nevertheless

and with every act of creation
you call upon the offspring of memory

Others may argue legend
and divide into cults

as if the daughters of gods
need their recognition

but something before
language and logic

high in the mountains
holds you

while your heart sings
to please heaven and earth

Assumption Day

The late afternoon sun is bearable
and the shallows
have had hours to heat
At least that's the theory

At the far edge of the inlet
we find space for personality
and room to loosen our limbs
in the angled glow

We set up camp
midway between
probable death
and prematurely wet towels

I wonder what emotions
the creatures
that make up these cliffs
enjoyed

and ponder whether
there's an ancestor
compacted
within the sediment

Skiers skim the surface of the bay
back and forth
going nowhere
purely for the experience

A man rows a dinghy
along the same stretch
for the same reason
his wife's face unimpressed

Waist high in seawater Johnny
waves his arms in delight
conducting the universe
to his very own score

In search of, but not expecting, awe

Tourists top the circular escarpment
like small figures on a wedding cake

The solar grill
barbecues my shoulders

A northerly air-conditions
my midriff

Ranks of surfers advance on waves
like foot soldiers

I guard towels as though regimental colours
whilst my son kicks up a vortex

White seahorses
soar overhead

A hipster with a papoose
reads as he mooches in the shallows

The arrangement of the ocean
calls to memory

Looking closely at my face in the past

There's someone else in my kitchen
He's younger than me
He's wearing my clothes
His hair still has colour

He is fooling himself with organic soup
and orange juice
The declaration 'free' is turned from his sight
The word 'pure' is there to be found

Holding on to white bread in his left hand
In his right, steel reflects light
The palette of the sun and sky
appears pale

The world around him seems out of focus
His head bowed
eyes closed
as if in prayer

From this angle I can see he is not alone
Does he feel the same as I do?
Does he know it's all going to be alright?
Does he even know that?

There are strangers in our garden

I'm sitting with us
from twenty-five years ago
in the shade of a single oak tree
with two trunks

Opposite
over the tallest elms
a twin engine
double underlines the sky

Two magpies
having no hands
brave their faces
to the dirt

The divide between
sunshine
and shadow
seems almost tangible

Standing on Dad's empty grave

Only his name next door
on mum's stone marks him

She died at 38, he at 90

I wonder what words
they'd have for each other

He chose to lie elsewhere

ashes at a crematorium
by the trade entrance

motivated by re-marriage

Disjointed in death
yet at some point someone

purchased both plots

Will this piece of ground
remain half vacant

double bed with an empty pillow

I wonder if they're re-united
without distraction

where everything falls away but   truth

Bracing

The wind makes pennants of our shirts
and threatens to swipe my cap

If I squint my right eye
I can see clear across this southern cove

The surface of the sea is loose
A kite karate chops the beach

Sand in my suntan lotion
provides an exfoliant

A man and his son flirt with the far edge
of the abandoned jetty

its concrete blocks now weathered
to blend with the scree

Originally built for sardine fishermen
now leisure has become the sole industry

Neither bluster nor potholes
can hold back the khaki tide

Umbrellas fringe the foot
of the western rise

like medieval shields
clustered against enemy archers

A sudden surge can blow your ice lolly
clean off its stick

The day before a birthday

The sea shines
as if someone has used a filter

There's a baby being carried in a shawl
one pink leg dangling in the sun

a man paddling a surf board kneels
as though in prayer

Half submerged
Johnny makes cheap sunglasses cool

he eyes the noisiest kids
in the immediate vicinity

His mother is always first
to dip her shoulders

The further away the headlands
the paler they become

A bikini girl struts the catwalk
clutching her iPod

Hand in hand a young couple
stroll the shoreline topless

A pregnant woman
corrals her previous babies

I settle into my notebook
a poem older

Another circuit almost complete

The open-faced balaclava

Bring back the balaclava
there's nothing suaver
like a scarf with a hat
but less palaver than that

Don't reserve it for skiing
it's for general wellbeing
a head-sock with a hole in
especially for seeing
though this helmet may well sweat
there's no disagreeing

Circulation revivers for arctic survivors
embracing the face of racing drivers
they keep out cold for deep sea divers

sported by astronauts or cops at airports
people with warts and spots of all sorts

For any cold snap on the weather map
try this templar cap with a front facing gap
that's the chap you should seek to unwrap
It's cosy headgear for all folks to wear

Knitted, fitted
friend of the zitted
ears with warmth benefitted
helps avoid viruses being transmitted
worn back to front if you're not that quick-witted

These woolly ballies
are not just for scallies
and should never be viewed
as a downmarket snood
or even meaner
a poor man's pashmina

An ushanka
no thank ya

for headgear to wear I'd much rather
go no farther
than pull on a woollen balaclava

I don't like throwing any photo away

Breathless
I am daunted by absence

Overwhelmed by fragility
and the world in your eyes
A sacred intimacy of light and presence

I don't like throwing any photo away
however blurred
damaged or faded

it's hard to let the moment go
it all seems so precious
so finite

The failing light catches the top of the palms

The middle-sized tree on the left
stands alone

The taller and the shorter tree on the right
are at arm's length

You could consider them a family
the smallest being the child

although with the height of children these days
maybe the tallest is the son

Bird-shapes bounce along terracotta
northern slopes cooler on claws

There is a risk of mosquitos
but tonight the ocean enchants

The cliff face is illuminated
like a friend to the moon

Over the mountains
there's a halo of burnt ochre

Centred

Too many people have hidden away
as though their pain only deserved shadow

as though their mother and father
never dreamt of light

as though their ancestors
hadn't loved and died in darkness

as though generation after generation
hadn't wept the clouds dry

as though life itself should cower

not today
this is where I make a stand

today, I create the universe
the sun can revolve around me

One half of the moon in the late afternoon

Hanging foolishly in the east
this pale imitation is universally ignored

by holiday makers
busy making holidays

orientated as usual
to the summer sun

A smudge of white
like a semi-circular cloud

has nowhere to hide
in the perfect blue

A buoy
in a sea with no boats

it is without purpose
other than for poets

and other lost souls

21st century urban peasant poetry manifesto

This poetry is:

1. the butter on the toast merging with the beans

2. recognising your father's face in the mirror

3. the smile that greets a stranger

4. the bearing of pain in the muscle

5. the child that stands back up

6. a whisper from the bathroom overheard

7. the kiss on a lover's forehead

8. scars under a long-sleeved shirt

9. the candle lit by the sceptic

10. unlikely to take itself too seriously, fat face

Winter Solstice

Droplets of dew shine silver
on the backs of our sun loungers
like stars hiding from morning

Olive leaves soften the ground
far too early
for Easter

Night storms and floods
become memory
as healing begins

Time slows, stretches
and curves
around my shape

Midday
finds its lowest angle
and caresses the north

My mother-in-law
sits in shade
for fear of cancer

There are colder climes
and more urgent concerns
elsewhere I know

Most clouds
don't cover the sun
and tend to go unnoticed

The Earth is over 4.5 billion years old

To cheer myself I can't resist
if I'm ever feeling fatigue
to remember that I managed to exist
at the same time as the Premier League

Climate change protests

Kids are concerned at the rise of the sea
much more than most men and women
They'll not suffer from skipping a lesson or three
unless the lesson they're skipping is swimming

Why not put solar panels on your roof?

When the National Grid is decimated
in a post-apocalyptic wrath
with the whole of society devastated
you can still have a nice hot bath

I have spent many years hiding from Christmas

The ocean never closes
It makes a land grab
towards my sandals

In wetsuit, cap and sunglasses
Johnny is the most chilled guy in Luz
even, no especially with, ear defenders

He claps and dances like a seal
as the Atlantic splutters
to keep up

The surface of this ice water
is shinier than any
manmade decoration

Angela is as patient
as a saint bearing gifts
though without the beard

(and the girth
I should add
though who knows after dinner)

Beneath feathered streamers
and a golden bauble
our soles sink into glossy sand

Dragging my chair
out of reach of the tide
I have drawn a line

Slow song of the baby sloth

I will lick my mother's lips to learn what to eat
I will digest my food at the slowest rate
usually I'm more leaf than meat
as much as two-thirds of my bodyweight

I will watch the world upside down
my coat will be adorned in algae
I have poor sight and hear little sound
my defence – to be part of the greenery

I am helpless on the ground but I can swim
Forty minutes underwater I can hold my breath
I'm the only animal named after a sin
I can remain hanging even after death

We sloths nourish moths that exist solely on us
biting and blood-sucking flies
lice, ticks, mites and bugs
When we do move it's mostly at night

For five months I will stay with my mother
I will die if I fall from this canopy
I can't ever expect help from another
not even a parent will heed my plea

I will urinate and defecate about every seven days
I will go to the same spot each time although
digging a hole in earth then covering it away
I'm vulnerable to predators while doing so

By burying my excreta near the trunk of my tree
I'll nourish this cecropia and it'll in turn nourish me
Moths, which live in my fur, will leave
to lay their eggs in my faeces

Larvae will hatch and on those faeces they'll feed
Mature they'll fly up and on my flesh proceed

For most of my life I'll lie motionless in fear
this way I may live past my twentieth year

Distant mist lies on the sea like a spectre

Invading the land opposite
                it claws its way up the cliff

Becoming dirty grey
                it throws itself upon the obelisk
                                        at the summit
then   di s s   i   p   a   t   e   s

as if
even the dead can commit suicide

This continues far longer than seems
feasible
but only in one small corner of creation

All   about
the sky is as blue as a swimming pool

How God was born

A group of spirits
couldn't remember
when they were young

so they decided to invent
a way to help them
find what was lost

They summoned light
and substance
and fashioned a universe

This universe was so vast
and existed for so long
that eventually new life appeared

This life evolved
and the spirits watched and prayed
that it would restore their memory

Into this universe
a baby was born
and it cried

And it looked to the heavens
for understanding
and the spirits cried

Stock Tunnocks
chocs for all stomachs
spoil us
silver and red foil us

I may plead and harangue
but I need my meringue
sitting on shortbread
to support the aforesaid

Don't approx a lummox
causing shocks and flummox
Be smart fox not dumb ox
Stock boxes and boxes of Tunnocks

The honey bucket

"Kings and philosophers shit, and so do ladies" – *Michel de Montaigne*

Even those with rounded vowels
cannot confound compounded bowels
let your food unfurl
celebrate 'the morning curl'

Every sovereign born to rule
through their ass did 'pass a stool'
'dropped the kids at the swimming pool'

Every potentate
upon a po did defecate
to 'cook up some sausages'
'negotiate release of hostages'

Each of the mighty Czars
'unloaded a batch of fine cigars'
left the toilet humming
engaged in 'scatter bombing'

Even the Queen must 'feed the vultures'
'make some underwater sculptures'
or in the woods like the proverbial bear
'download some software'

No top knob's too snob to bob
Every President without fail
is obliged 'to make a tail'

Still the image that most lingers
is Putin 'making gorilla fingers'

Found alive and well and living in obscurity

Didn't you used to be someone?
You left us all nonplussed
I always wondered where you'd gone
Did you jump or were you pushed?

Whatever happened to you?
I remember you much fitter
What was that thing you used to do
before it went down the shitter?

So you're not dead then?
I'd heard that you'd just freaked
Good to see you alive again
I'll never forget that day you peaked

Once I thought you might make it
was your decline due to ill health?
No, now I come to think of it
I've mistook you for someone else

Where skeletal cats sleep under rusty cars

Beautiful as it is
the Atlantic is as cold as meltwater

A man with a whistle and sunglasses
patrols the over-populated sand

Three young kids balance
on a single surfboard

A youth with his arm in a sling
still plays football with his mates

A toddler sporting nothing but armbands
splashes in two inches of froth

Johnny enrobed with towel
enthroned on striped canvas

demands his feet be entombed
then resurrects them

in far less time
than it takes to bury the buggers

Angela drip dries
as the ocean evaporates on her skin

We are no longer
the whitest people in Portugal

High clouds line up like
semi-quavers

Only tiny trunks in the public pool
the French law decrees
No baggy shorts is the rule
No cool breeze round your testes

So much for 'The Land of the Free'
This liberty they've taken since 1903

For the home of haute cuisine doth legislate
your meat and two veg be served on a plate

In the Republic of the Tricolour
they're a stickler for this particular
on matters testicular

To be frank it's a Franco-failure
this highlighting of male genitalia

Bather beware when wearing Speedos
'Curb Your Libido'
needs to be your credo
so's not to be perceived
as a perv or a paedo

To indulge a bulge – bon
To own a boner – non

You Gauls have got some gall
with your apparel to appal
You sneer at us
'all this fuss
over something so small'

It's hardly haute couture
Not my idea of a package tour
Not for me – for sure
I don't like it clingy
round my thingy
non merci monsieur

'Stay in the UK' you may well say
'if you don't want your dipstick on display'
but in the land of La Marseillaise
budgie smugglers s'il vous plaît

We French believe it's not so bad
to see the curve of the odd gonad

Yes you can mock
our Gallic cock
our briefs like a banana hammock

But you'll never ban 'le slip de bain'
snug as though sprayed from a can

We'll never admit too tight a fit
so you can put a sock in it

Vive la France
capital of romance
we wear our hearts
in our skimpy pants

Unless ironically
and here's the rub
you're in the tub
of how you say
a private members' club

My hair has gone on ahead

I wonder how much hair
has been cut from my head

What length it would it be now
if I'd left it instead

Would its ends still be blond
the middle bit brown

the roots faded grey
white at the crown

A colour coded record
of my life passing

not scattered landfill
still amassing

In Memoriam – Henry Normal

Henry Normal died earlier today
writing his own obituary
Found slumped so they say
over a rhyming dictionary

Details of his death – no shit too scary
have been released – though bits do vary
Police refuse to – omit new theory
He died trying to rhyme – obituary
and in the end did – vomit blueberry

It's how he would have wanted to go
all who knew him agreed
His poetry is haunted though
claim those who have since heard him read

We will never see his 'like' again
His similes have all gone south
mixed metaphors and mismatching metre that flowed from his
    pen
can no longer fly like pigs from his mouth

Some are sad at his loss
Some don't give a toss
Some are happy bec'os
they won't come across any more of his dross

Mostly remembered for his lack of looks
and his passion to avoid expense
He leaves behind a stack of books
all reduced to 72 pence

Two wise men in the Algarve

The gates to Heaven are padlocked
Jesus is out celebrating his birthday
There's a dog with three legs
who has to sit down to scratch
A jogger in a Santa hat challenges the beach
A couple in bathers play bat and ball
while Christians sing in their best topcoats

And 'me and Johnny'
in jumpers and sunglasses
at the recycling bins
with an empty bottle of port
save the world
having burnt fossil fuel
for two hours to get here

Lent, but the charm is giving up nothing

Don't be fooled by the name
even the goldfinch itself
is red faced

its heart racing
with each nervous tick
like it's in the wrong poem

it hangs from a birdfeeder
a domestic crucifix
with caged seed

its movements jerky
its wings strobe
a fighter jet with Tourette's

it flits and darts
its song sharp
an eat seeking missile

never quite set
it snatches
its mid-morning snack

Under this dirty sky
spring pushing through
bright yellow can suffice

for gold

The lost arrow

My welcome is unassuming
instilled from first smack
there is no need for ceremony amongst kin
as if to say I will see your face again
this is where we are, this is who we are
this is who we will be when next we meet

There is matter-of-factness to this heritage
borne from the legacy of human industry
the early morning bus to Raleigh Island
the truth of hard work done well
openness unbowed and easy civility
warmth in the most cutting of winds

Slab Square is where I celebrate
centred yet embracing change
I breathe to the pace of a northern boulevard
my veins run Forest red
I carry Nottingham in my bones
it will outlast this temporary flesh

I have a hand-crafted sense of self
individual yet part of something solid
from red brick terrace to green estate
from Bread and Lard Island to the Park
I have lived this old city in all its seasons
loved and ached and mourned at every kerb

My accent is in the architecture
in the unsung history of its pavements
in the immediacy of a Saturday night
in the friendliness to strangers
my soles have worn on these streets
my dreams taken flight under this sky

In the eyes of the grande
I may have little
but what I have is mine
assured with a quiet defiance
I carry Nottingham in my bones
nothing under heaven can take it away

Local headlines

A car with crumpled
bonnet drives slowly and with
care after the fact

Open-top sports not
aware they're trailing a branch
trapped in the door

Man with walking stick
wears new trainers to catch the
departing Sprinter

Poet outside church
inspired as summer rain
softens the new page

It seems like the sun has been self-isolating

On today's one outing for exercise
from Seaford Head to Cuckmere Haven

I stop, as always, by my brother's bench
overlooking the Seven Sisters

It's warm enough to walk but not to settle

Lambs stay close to their mother
without need for social distancing

People pass each other
on the opposite side of the path

no one is in a hurry
we have time to kill or be killed

We are the only thing in this landscape
the virus can thrive on

Nature will shed no tears for us

Angela says sadly
a generation after her death
no-one will remember her

You will live on in my poetry
I try to console her, half joking, but only half

She looks at me as if to suggest
my poetry may not outlast either of us

Crocuses are emerging on cue
as though no-one has told them otherwise

home schooling

again, when I wake
for a moment all is well
then I remember

I reduce ambition and expectation
find the lowest gear

draw out morning routines
my house has never been so clean

it's hard to remember which day it is
they're losing names and becoming numbers

always dress down Friday
in a month of Sundays

we exist in unfashionable slippers
we live on screens of all sizes

stir crazy – I drink tea on draught
wash my hands like my life depended on it

exercise once a day
being once more a day than I'm used to

wrap myself against nature
lay my clothes fallow to avoid the wash

each week I chance the supermarket
stand in the dotted line

over a breath away
the length of a hospital bed

negotiate the aisles
turn my back to the space invaders

I'm resorting to DIY
sorting corners to make my home bigger

spraying the tops of taps again,
keys, door knobs again and again

resisting the itch on my face
hands like deadly weapons

using elbows and feet to open and close doors
leaving packages and letters in quarantine

experimenting with available ingredients
toasting the last of the bread

seeing how many cups I can get from a tea bag
the least amount of toilet paper per visit

I watch the news too long then try and find
a little escape to improve my dreams

I'm wary of every cough or sneeze, every ache
careful not to stay up late in case it lowers resistance

I treasure
I appreciate

I empathise until it hurts
I close my eyes

again, when I wake
for a moment all is well
then I remember

In shade birds are whistling up their dinner

Insects are having a field day

Flies become familiar
no respecters of social distancing

A ladybird lands on my lapel
like a brooch

Bumblebees drunk on oxygen
zigzag over bluebells

as though they know
something even smaller than them
now rules the Earth

Avoiding a second wave by keeping the first going

Trinity Sunday and the seasons turn
from spring to summer
a purple clematis sunbathes
even the chives stand ready

As lush as the garden is
there are still old leaves
lingering in the beech trees
like abandoned cocoons

Curls of dry foliage
cling to inner branches
like faded memories
as though unable to part

Pages from a scorched diary
perhaps hoping to hide
until autumn offers
the solace of company

Liberation – a hai(five)ku

My own personal
flyby on this VE day
a real Tiger Moth

Aphids hover like
small Chinook helicopters
patrolling the grass

A seagull opens
its bomb doors over my shed
marking its target

A cross stands empty
My scarecrow has left its post
a sign to nowhere

Alliums salute
wisteria and bluebells
greet like lost cousins

My son tells me he can hear flowers moving

A couple of pale pink tulips
whisper
at the foot of the pergola

Nearer the house scarlet petals
like the points of a star
pull the eye

The olive trees
are beginning
to take shape

Pure white daffodils
refuse to die
today

Delicate blossom
on the pear tree
seems unassuming

There are lighter greens
on the smaller leaves
and twigs becoming two-tone

Though overlooked before
due to scale
small shoots scab the soil

If I concentrate on a single flower
it's difficult to understand
how anything could be more beautiful

Virus? What virus?

Under uninfected blue
lying amongst lazy insects

cushions in the hammock
blanket on the grass

locked down in the moment
the April sun warms pale skin

Today the cleaning of surfaces
has gone out the window

Outside the beauty of the magnolia is burned by the wind

For now
we are house plants

safe from the late winter

eking out sunlight
through closed windows

drinking cool water
and waiting for summer

when we hope
doors will open

and a warm breeze
reunite us

with a gentler nature

I-solation-ku x 2 – a love poem

When I sit alone
it still feels better knowing
you are in the world

When I lay my head
upon my pillow to sleep
you are all my dreams

Amongst mayflies

Sun warming my face
I pass these precious hours
breathing to the pace
of wild flowers

Unselfish isolation

Angela's worried about Coronavirus
she wants to do her bit
she says she's prepared to self-isolate
together with Brad Pitt

73% H$_2$O

We are drawn to water
in all her glories
from the great open ocean
to a communal pool
to the edge of a small park lake

Perhaps because
we are built from flood
each carried into this world submerged
a connection as strong as tide
the ripples of 'a warm little pond'

That most ancient element of light
bonds twice
to the breath of all living creatures
and the story of our creation
springs

Through fluidity
and salted flow
we are carried down the generations
on storms
back to the oldest sea

Drench us in understanding
quench our keenest thirst
then
wrench us like a whirlpool
and immerse us in one another

Not my cup of tea

As a connoisseur I like a brew
but even at a push
Rooibos in my mush won't do

Assam – no thank you ma'am
I'm happy as I am goddamn

Darjeeling – not a char I find appealing
leaves me far from a nice warm feeling

Camomile – don't make me smile
I'd run a mile before I drink that bile

Oolong just tastes wrong
so does Lapsang Souchong

To save confusion
I'd add exclusion
of any organic fruit infusion

Herbal Tea – not for me
Ginseng – not my thing
Earl Grey – no way Jose
Green decaf – not keen too naff
Masala Chai – I'd rather die
Salted Caramel – fucking terrible

Whether square bags, pyramid or round
Salted Caramel tastes shit I've found
Those with perforations
taste like abominations

Loose leaf
offers little relief

No, for me it's – English Breakfast
a distinguished tea you wanna meck last
or if in a hurry – easily neck fast

Quickly done – never too tricky
with sticky bun or chockie bicky

It's the Daddie in the caddie
it's the pot that hits the spot

Snug in a mug or a bone china cup
chug on that drug – there's no finer sup

Sipping PG Tips through my lips
I could even enjoy the apocalypse

It's the beverage
for whatever age

same with Tetley or Yorkshire
most of the rest are just plain torture

Co-op Home Brand?
That'll be grand

Locking down

It's not even June
and the lawn is as dry as old paper

the wild roses show wild ambition
stretching out to trees beyond reach

we look for permanence
in a universe we know will end

stability in a world
we know is in flux

consistency in a reality
that is ever changing

reliability in a life
that we know owes us nothing

writing these poems is perhaps
an excuse to sit still for longer

I tip the barnacled glass
with its blisters of colour
and let the soup
e x p l o d e
into the kitchen sink

bright white is suddenly
dashed with purple/brown
as the s pl a tt e r pattern
stretches its fingers
to all sides of the hollow cube

then turning the tap
the paint swirls
th in n i n g to dusky pink
around the stainless-steel rim
of the plughole into the black

Stabs of scarlet and gold
spark like small fireworks
as I bend the brushes
against the porcelain
and droplets dilut e

Wiping with a sponge
the wash s p   r   e   a   d s
and tints until
the last smears disappear
and the basin returns
to a shining blank canvas

Circling back

Even as we leave
on our daily exercise
we are heading home

Infected sleep

I'm travelling more
in nightmares than when awake
my mind won't lockdown

Spare room

Grandma's and Grandad's
dressing gowns still hang waiting
unworn and forlorn

Slippers in the garden – civilisation has officially collapsed

Jasmine has come and gone unnoticed
upstaged by the news

I can hear home-locked kids
playing in the long grass next door

and diggers on a distant building site
laying the foundations of a new home

The coast road traffic is now intermittent
and somehow more noticeable because of it

A few insects seem to have woken
and are trying to propagate my mustard cardie

Blood red tulips are social distancing
Apple blossom appears a little shy

Easter
lurks somewhere in the forgotten calendar

The sun skims a continent of cloud
Primroses edge the small path

A bumblebee achieves the impossible

Lightning before death

The music is not made in the radio
it comes from elsewhere

The mind is not seen on an X-ray
Who are we to say there's no spirit?

Let me whisper a final farewell
remind you of who I once was

More than biology and chemistry
more than mere physics

someone individual
something unique

If I linger in your thoughts
it's this part of me that stays

It was always the part
that was me

connecting with the part
that is you

The escape plan

Have no doubt
I write these poems for you

These words are an oath
An incantation

Have no doubt
I will come to you
when you are most in need

I will love you
as though you are my younger self

Have no doubt
I will find you

and we will escape together